Olympic Technology

Elapsed Time

John Lockyer

Publishing Credits

Editor
Sara Johnson

Editorial Director
Emily R. Smith, M.A.Ed.

Editor-in-Chief
Sharon Coan, M.S.Ed.

Creative Director
Lee Aucoin

Publisher
Rachelle Cracchiolo, M.S.Ed.

Image Credits

The authors and publisher would like to gratefully credit or acknowledge the following for permission to reproduce copyright material: Cover Getty Images/Adrian Dennis reproduced with permission of Chris Hoy; p.1 Getty Images/Stu Forster; p.4 Getty Images/Romeo Gacad; p.5 Getty Images/Michael Steele; p.6 Getty Images/Frederic J. Brown; p.7 Getty Images; p.8 International Olympic Committee; p.9 (top) Getty Images/Paul Gilham; p.9 (centre) Getty Images/Chris McGrath; p.9 (bottom) Science Photo Library; p.10 International Olympic Committee; p.11 Getty Images/Carl de Souza; p.12 Getty Images; p.13 Getty Images/Romeo Gacad; p.13 (inset) Getty Images/Tobias Titz; p.14 Alamy; p.15 Getty Images/David Cannon; p.16 Getty Images; p.17 AAP Image; p.18 Getty Images; p.19 (top) Alamy; p.19 (bottom) Getty Images/Simon Bruty; p.20 Getty Images/Nat Farbman; p.21 Getty Images/Mark Dadswell; p.22 (top) Getty Images/George Marks; p.22 (bottom) Getty Images; p.23 Getty Images/Nicolas Asfouri; p.24 Getty Images/Al Bello; p.25 Getty Images/Julian Finney; p.26 (top) Photolibrary.com; p.26 (center) International Olympic Committee; p.26 (bottom) Getty Images; p.27 (top) Getty Images/David Cannon; p.27 (bottom) Getty Images/Romeo Gacad; p.29 AAP Image/Anja Niedringhaus.

While every care has been taken to trace and acknowledge copyright, the publishers tender their apologies for any accidental infringement where copyright has proved untraceable. They would be pleased to come to a suitable arrangement with the rightful owner in each case.

Teacher Created Materials
5301 Oceanus Drive
Huntington Beach, CA 92649-1030
http://www.tcmpub.com

ISBN 978-0-7439-0901-3

Table of Contents

Be Your Best

The Olympic Summer Games has a **motto**: Higher—Faster—Stronger. This means that all Olympic athletes should try to do their very best.

Better sports **technology** (tek-NOL-uh-jee) helps athletes reach their goals. Today, they jump higher, run faster, and throw farther than ever before.

An athlete competing in the 2004 Athens Olympic Games

What Is Technology?

Athletes use technology to improve their performances with better **equipment**. When you want to improve something, learn all about it and then see if you can use technology to make it better.

The modern Olympic Summer Games began in Greece in 1896. Only men took part in them. The very first event was a 100-meter sprint. The winning time for the final was 12.0 seconds. Thanks to better sports technology, 100 years later the winning time was 9.84 seconds!

In 2008, Jamaican runner Usain Bolt set a new world and Olympic record for the men's 100-meter sprint — 9.69 seconds.

LET'S EXPLORE MATH

The first modern Olympic Games were held in Athens in 1896.

a. How many years have passed since the first modern Olympics?

b. Describe the **strategy** you used to solve this problem.

Sports Technology

There are many things athletes do to perform at their best. They eat a healthy diet. They train hard. Coaching is also very important.

Some athletes start training when they are very young.

LET'S EXPLORE MATH

An athlete must train many hours each day to prepare for the Olympic Games. Luca, a swimmer, has to train in the pool for $3\frac{1}{2}$ hours in the morning and $2\frac{1}{4}$ hours in the afternoon. If Luca started training at 5:20 A.M. and at 3:40 P.M., what time would he finish each session?

5:20 A.M.

3:40 P.M.

Sports technology also helps athletes. Today, athletes wear better clothing than athletes long ago. Shoes and equipment have improved. The **venues** (VEN-youz) where athletes compete are better. And the tools used to measure times have changed.

A runner crosses the finish line in the 1960 Games in Rome, Italy.

Cathy Freeman wore a hooded bodysuit at the 2000 Games in Sydney, Australia.

Clothing

Swimsuits

Swimsuits have changed a lot since the 1896 Athens Olympics. Back then, swimsuits were made with wool. This made them very heavy when wet. Swimmers were weighed down in the water.

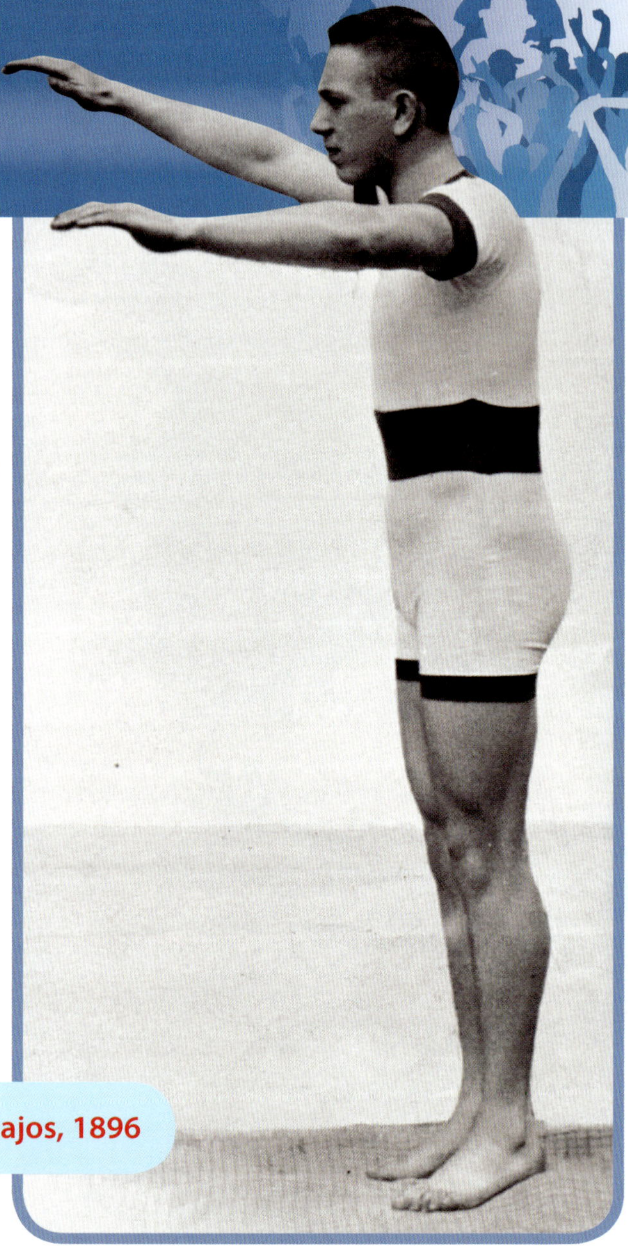

Alfréd Hajos, 1896

Winning Times — Then and Now

Olympic Games	Athlete	Swimming Event	Winning Time
1896 Athens	Alfréd Hajos, Hungary	100-meter freestyle	1 minute 22 seconds
2008 Beijing	Alain Bernard, France	100-meter freestyle	47.21 seconds

Technology has improved swimsuits. Today, they are made from very light **fabrics**. Water can flow easily over them, so swimmers are not slowed down in the water.

Like many swimmers at the Beijing Olympics, Alain Bernard wore a swimsuit made out of special fabric.

Swimming in Shark Skin

Some Olympic swimsuits have tiny "v-shaped" **ridges** on them. This is like shark skin. These ridges help the water flow across swimmers' bodies, without slowing them down.

Cycling Clothes

Cyclists in the 1896 Athens Olympic Games wore heavy, baggy woolen shorts. These shorts caught the wind and slowed down the cyclists. Back then, cyclists did not wear helmets.

Paul Masson, 1896

Winning Times — Then and Now

Olympic Games	Athlete	Cycling Event	Winning Time
1896 Athens	Paul Masson, France	2,000-meter sprint	4 minutes 58 seconds
2004 Athens	Chris Hoy, Great Britain	1-kilometer time trial	1 minute

Technology has improved the clothing cyclists wear. Today, cyclists have special bodysuits that are made from light fabrics. They are very tight. This helps cyclists ride faster than ever before.

Their helmets are light and curved. Air moves easily over them so they do not slow cyclists down.

At the 2008 Games, Chris Hoy won 3 gold medals.

LET'S EXPLORE MATH

In 1896, a French cyclist won the 2,000-meter sprint in 4 minutes and 58 seconds.

a. If the race started at 2:50 P.M., at what time did he finish?

b. Explain how you solved this problem. Then explain another approach to solving this problem.

Shoes

In the 1896 Athens Olympic Games, athletes wore track shoes made from leather. The shoes had long spikes in the soles. This helped the runner grip the track. But these shoes stretched after a while. They became loose. It was hard for athletes to run fast in them.

The Olympic 100-meter sprint, 1896

Winning Times — Then and Now

Olympic Games	Athlete	Running Event	Winning Time
1896 Athens	Tom Burke, U.S.A	Men's 100-meter sprint	12 seconds
1988 Seoul	Florence Griffith Joyner, U.S.A	Women's 100-meter sprint	10.62 seconds

Technology has improved track shoes. Today, they are made from light fabrics. They do not stretch. They have small spikes at the front. The athletes do not need to use a lot of energy to lift their feet. So they have more energy to run fast.

Florence Griffith Joyner, 1988, still holds the Olympic Record time in the women's 100-meter sprint.

Equipment

Bicycles

Early bicycles were made of **steel**. They weighed more than 45 pounds (20.4 kg). The handlebars were high. The wheels had spokes. This caused lots of wind resistance. Olympic cyclists had to use a lot of energy to ride these heavy bikes. No wonder their times were slower than Olympic cyclists today.

Technology has improved bicycles. Today, they are made of very light materials. In the 1992 Barcelona Olympic Games, cyclist Chris Boardman rode a "super bike." It weighed only 17.6 pounds (8 kg). It had low handlebars. The front wheel only had 3 spokes and the back wheel had none. With this amazing bike, Chris Boardman set new Olympic Games records. Technology still changes bikes today.

Chris Boardman on the racing bike he used in the 1992 Games

LET'S EXPLORE MATH

At the 2000 Sydney Olympic Games, a cross-country cycling race started at 1:00 P.M. The gold medalist crossed the finish line at 3:09:05 P.M. The bronze medalist crossed the line 2 minutes and 16 seconds later.

a. How long did the gold medalist take to complete the course?

b. At what time did the bronze medalist cross the line?

The Pole Vault

In the pole vault, athletes use long poles to jump over a high bar. Early poles were made out of **bamboo**. Athletes flew high over the bar, then they landed on their feet in a pile of sawdust.

Bamboo poles were last used in the 1948 London Olympic Games.

Owen Guinn Smith, 1948

Winning Heights — Then and Now

Olympic Games	Athlete	Event	Winning Height
1948 London	Owen Guinn Smith, U.S.A	Men's pole vault	4.3 meters
2008 Beijing	Yelena Isinbaeva, Russia	Women's pole vault	5.05 meters

Today, the poles are light but strong. They are made of **fiberglass** or **carbon fiber**. They bend well. This helps the athletes jump higher than before. And today, the athletes have a softer landing. They land on a thick foam mat.

Yelena Isinbaeva, 2008

LET'S EXPLORE MATH

A pole vault competition finished at 3:40 P.M. The whole competition lasted 1 hour and 15 minutes.

a. At what time did the competition start?

b. Describe how you solved this problem.

Surfaces

Track

Long ago, athletes ran on tracks made from **cinders** or crushed stone. These tracks were bumpy. Sometimes the runners slipped. In the 1936 Berlin Olympic Games, an American runner ran the 100-meter sprint on a track made of cinders. He wore leather shoes and floppy shorts. Yet he ran an amazing time and won the gold medal.

American Jesse Owens, 1936 winner of the men's 100-meter sprint

Winning Times — Then and Now

Olympic Games	Athlete	Running Event	Winning Time
1936 Berlin	Jesse Owens, U.S.A	Men's 100-meter sprint	10.3 seconds
2008 Beijing	Usain Bolt, Jamaica	Men's 100-meter sprint	9.69 seconds

Technology has improved running tracks. In the 1968 Mexico City Olympic Games, a new track was used for the first time. It was called a *Tartan track*. It was made of a special rubber. This new track was smooth and flat. Athletes could run faster without slipping. Tartan tracks are still used today.

A Tartan track

Usain Bolt, 2008

Field Hockey

Field hockey is played by people from many countries around the world. Field hockey has been played at almost every Olympic Games since 1908. Up until the early 1970s, field hockey was played on grass. Grass was bumpy and slowed down the hockey ball.

In many nations around the world, this sport is known as hockey.

LET'S EXPLORE MATH

In a field hockey match, there are two halves that are each 35 minutes. There is also a 10-minute break at halftime.

a. If a field hockey game between China and Australia started at 3:10 P.M., what time would it finish?

b. Describe how you solved this problem.

Technology has changed field hockey. Today, it is played on **artificial** (are-tuh-FISH-uhl) turf. This surface was first used at the 1976 Games in Montreal, Canada. Turf fields are smooth, and the hockey ball can roll much faster.

Around the world, men and women play field hockey on artificial turf.

An Ancient Game

Field hockey is one of the world's oldest ball and stick games. Records show that a form of the game was played in Persia (now Iran) in 2000 B.C.

Timing

At the Track

In 1896, people used stopwatches to record track athletes' times. Stopwatches were still being used at the 1932 Los Angeles Olympic Games. Many different people timed the track events "by hand" to figure out the finishing times.

Time-keepers record the results of a race at the 1932 Games.

Technology has changed the way Olympic track events are timed. Computers are now used. There is a laser beam at the finish line of track races. As athletes cross the line, they block the beam. This sends signals to computers. The computers record the times.

Athletes cross the finish line in a race at the 2008 Games.

LET'S EXPLORE MATH

You want to watch the women's marathon on television. The race starts at 6:45 P.M. The winning time is 2 hours, 26 minutes, and 20 seconds. Your bedtime is 9:00 P.M. Will you be able to see the end of the race?

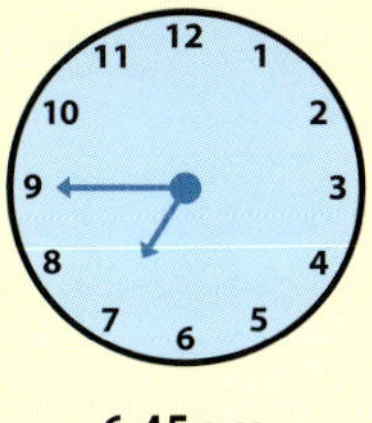

6:45 P.M.

Swimming and Cycling

Olympic bicycles have **transmitters** on their front wheels. The transmitters record their times. The times are sent to computers. Cameras are also set up at the finish line. They take photos of the race finish.

Olympic swimming blocks have **sensors** in them. They record when a swimmer dives off the block. Olympic pools have touch pads on their walls. They record when a swimmer touches the wall at the end of a race.

Swimmers touching the wall at the end of a race

LET'S EXPLORE MATH

In 2004 in Athens, the winning time for the 1,500-meter freestyle swimming race was 14 minutes 43 seconds. What was the finish time of the race if the starting time was 8:55 A.M.?

8:55 A.M.

Doing Their Best

Sports technology is very important. There seems to be no sport that technology cannot improve. Through sports technology and hard work, Olympic athletes can do their very best.

Swimming superstar Michael Phelps swam in 8 events and won 8 gold medals at the Beijing Olympic Games.

Olympic Time Line

776 B.C.	• The Olympic Games were first held in ancient Greece.
1896	• The first modern Olympic Games were held in Greece. • Alfréd Hajos of Hungry wins the 100-meter swimming final in a time of 1 minute 22 seconds. • Paul Masson of France wins the 2,000-meter cycling sprint in a time of 4 minutes 58 seconds. • Tom Burke of the U.S. wins the 100-meter sprint final in a time of 12.0 seconds.
1936	• Jesse Owens of the U.S. wins the 100-meter sprint final in a time of 10.3 seconds.
1948	• Owen Guinn Smith of the U.S. wins the men's pole vault with a jump of 4.3 meters.
1968	• Tartan track is used for the first time.

1976	• Field hockey is played on artificial turf for the first time.
1988	• Florence Griffith Joyner of the U.S. wins the women's 100-meter sprint final in an Olympic record time of 10.62 seconds.
1992	• Chris Boardman of Great Britain rides his "super bike" in Barcelona.
2000	• Cathy Freeman, an Aboriginal Australian, wins the women's 400-meter track final.
2008	• Michael Phelps, U.S. swimmer, wins a record 8 gold medals in 1 Olympic Games. • Usain Bolt of Jamaica wins the men's 100-meter sprint final in a world and Olympic record time of 9.69 seconds. • Yelena Isinbaeva of Russia wins the women's pole vault and holds the world and Olympic record jump of 5.05 meters.

Problem-Solving Activity

Seeing the Swimming

The Olympic Games are a very popular event for spectators. Jacinta has tickets to one of the swimming sessions, but she needs to find out what time she must leave home so she will not miss any of the races. The session will start at 10:00 A.M.

10:00 A.M.

Jacinta will take public transportation. She will walk to the bus stop, take a bus to the train station, take a train to the Olympic station, and walk from the station to the swimming venue.

- The walk from her home to the bus stop takes 9 minutes.
- The bus ride takes 35 minutes.
- She arrives at the station 6 minutes early.
- Jacinta catches the 8:55 A.M. train.
- The train trip takes 45 minutes.
- It takes Jacinta 20 minutes to walk from the Olympic station to the venue and find her seat.

Solve It!

What time does Jacinta have to leave her home? Use these steps to help you work out your answer.

Step 1: Write the time the session starts, so Jacinta knows what time she needs to be seated.

Step 2: Subtract the number of minutes it will take her to walk from the Olympic station to the venue.

Step 3: Subtract the time the train trip takes, then the waiting time at the station, then the bus trip time, and finally the time it takes her to walk to the bus stop.

Glossary

artificial—fake, not real

bamboo—a kind of light but strong, flexible wood

carbon fiber—threads of carbon that form a light, strong but flexible material

cinders—partly burnt coal

equipment—things needed for a sport

fabrics—material or cloth

fiberglass—fine threads of glass woven into a light, strong but flexible material

motto—a saying

ridges—bumps

sensors—devices that record movement

steel—a kind of metal

strategy—a method

technology—systems and equipment to help something work better

transmitters—devices that send and receive signals

venues—places where events are held

Index

ANSWER KEY

Let's Explore Math

Page 5:
a. Answers will vary.
b. Answers will vary.

Page 6:
Morning session: 5:20 + 3 hours = 8:20 + 30 minutes = 8:50 A.M.

Afternoon session: 3:40 + 2 hours = 5:40 + 15 minutes = 5:55 P.M.

Page 11:
a. Finish time: 2:50 + 4 minutes = 2:54 + 58 seconds = 2:54 P.M. and 58 seconds or 2:54:58 P.M.
b. Answers will vary.

Page 15:
a. 2 hours, 9 minutes and 5 seconds
b. The bronze medallist crossed the line at 3:11 P.M. and 21 seconds or 3:11:21 P.M.

Page 17:
a. The competition started at 2:25 P.M.
b. Answers will vary.

Page 20:
a. 35 minutes + 35 minutes + 10 minutes = 80 minutes = 1 hour 20 minutes
3:10 P.M.+ 1 hour = 4:10 P.M. + 20 minutes = 4:30 P.M.

The game would finish at 4:30 P.M.

b. Answers will vary.

Page 23:
6:45 P.M. + 2 hours = 8:45 P.M. + 26 minutes = 9:11 P.M. + 20 seconds = 9:11 P.M. and 20 seconds or 9:11:20 P.M.

You could not have seen the whole race.

Page 24:
8:55 A.M. + 5 minutes = 9:00 A.M. + 9 minutes = 9:19 A.M. + 43 seconds = 9:19 A.M. and 43 seconds or 9:19:43 A.M.

Problem-Solving Activity

Step 1: The session starts at 10:00 A.M.

Step 2: 10:00 – 20 minutes (walk from station to venue) = 9:40 A.M.

Step 3: 9:40 – 45 minutes (train trip) = 8:55 A.M.

8:55 – 6 minutes (wait at train station) = 8:49 A.M.

8:49 – 35 minutes (bus trip) = 8:14 A.M.

8:14 – 9 minutes (walk from home to bus) = 8:05 A.M.

Jacinta has to leave her home at 8:05 A.M.